BIRDS FOR ALL SEASONS

David Axtell

"So priketh hem nature in hir corages" (Chaucer)

ARTHUR H. STOCKWELL LTD
Torrs Park   Ilfracombe   Devon
Established 1898
www.ahstockwell.co.uk

British Library Cataloguing-in-Publication Data.
A catalogue record for this book is available
from the British Library.

ISBN 978-0-7223-3908-4
Printed in Great Britain by
Arthur H. Stockwell Ltd
Torrs Park Ilfracombe
Devon

For my wife and family

and to all those who love and care for birds

Contents

Spring

Summer

Autumn

Winter

SPRING

" the song thrush sits on the
highest branch "

Dawn Chorus

As the warmth returns to spring
And the days grow long,
In the early morning light
Birds fill the air with song.

To join the great tit's rocking sound,
The robin and the wren,
The song thrush sits on the highest branch
And sings each phrase again.

Green- and chaffinch join the throng,
Blackbird and dunnock too,
For right to forage and a mate
Their boldest notes renew.

The collared dove, which has its mate,
Croons with a gentler tone,
Warbler and chiffchaff may be heard
But the thrush retains the throne.

Birds in Spring

Birds are on overdrive in spring –
For food, a mate, a place to build,
From early dawn till late at night
The lawn's become a battlefield.

In a rage to replicate their genes
A war o'er territory they declare,
Proof of strength and right to claim
Assert with songs that fill the air.

At Night in Spring

Since birds may die 'fore morning comes
While still the cold remains,
When they're not engaged in song
They start to feed again.

Though in awareness less secure
And in what has gone before,
Not knowing what the skies may bring
They rest in instinct sure.

The Siskin

In the early days of spring,
Busily in search of minute seed
From branch to slender branch it drops.
I watch it delicately feed
Just 'neath the level of my eye,
Then to another tender hold it hops.
Brief visitor to my wall and hedges,
Silvery grey, not over-shy,
A bird of light and airy places,
Used to bouncing on branches' edges,
Soon to the north it will depart,
In dancing forest pines to breed.

Birds in Song

Birds with a will to live and breed
With cheerful song make hedgerows ring,
In choruses or solo airs
Make light of earthbound suffering.

The robin, which sings the whole year round,
As winter ends refines its skills,
The dunnock, too, its run prepares
Though more prosaic – no finishing frill.

The greenfinch sings between two showers,
With rise and fall its flute it plies,
Above the warbles, chirps and trills
For purity with the blackbird vies.

Starlings whistle, click and chirr
As, passing through, they rest on trees,
For resident birds show scant regard,
Mimic and practise vocalese.

Starlings massed, with many a wing
Make a single flutter as they shift their ground,
While a chaffinch boldly shakes its notes
And fills an empty lane with sound.

Waders on the water's edge
Lost times in elegies recall,
Flying overhead, with a single cluck,
A crow claims dominance over all.

But, of all the birds that sing
And for a place to live contest,
One with its repertoire, one its voice,
The thrush and the blackbird are the best.

SUMMER

" we watch him as he listens "

The Blackbird

He scuttles forth from flower bed
In Sunday best, at early dawn.
We watch him as he listens,
Makes a sudden run.
Other birds visit,
Starlings come and go,
A robin sits upon a spade,
Attends us while we dig or hoe.
But as light fades,
Before the curtain's drawn
We see him once again.
We but observe,
He is the tenant of the lawn.

The Seagulls

Flat-footed and gauche,
Well-fed and smug,
They stand on the roof's ridge,
A pair of gulls.
Others mock and wail,
Clamouring for food
They do not need.
A jackdaw stands his ground nearby
But they lord it over the rest.
Sparrows live a different life,
A bunch in a merry bush,
Flying to and fro
And finding enough
In tiny bits
To keep them in good chirrup.

Seagulls in Flight

The seagulls shine white in the early sun,
Catching the light against a 'drop* of grey,
Floating and casual in the rising air
Towards the sea they drift at break of day.

* backdrop

Blackbird's Song

Listen to the blackbird,
Its full-throated chirrup,
Oh, hear its true, glad
Waterfall of song,
Sweeter than syrup!

The Sparrowhawk

After the storm
The sun came out
And I heard a blackbird sing.
Its familiar song said –
"All is well.
I sing because 'tis so!"

Passing a window,
Some time spent,
Under a hedge I saw
A large and unfamiliar bird
I couldn't at first recall.

We all looked –
It was a sparrowhawk,
But then we saw its prey.
"It's a blackbird,"
Then said one of us.
On its back it lay.

And then I remembered
The blackbird's song
And wondered when it was
The killer struck
And took the life
That had brought so much joy.

The Quiet

The chestnut in the early sun
Is outside the sound of passing cars.
Visited by a solitary bee
Or briefly by a flight of birds,
It retains its separate quietness.
Geese, in the distance, fly over in a V,
Their sound belongs in the timeless still.
But the start of a motor,
To cut grass, or trim a hedge,
Disturbs not this other world.

The Blackbirds' Nest

With a trimmer, at the hedge,
Into their world I came,
Stripped branches, loudly,
In a moment, exposed to view
(A season's work undone)
Their nest and eggs.
The blackbirds had already fled
And from a distance watched,
Invisible to me.
Sparrows, their neighbours,
With noise and fluttering
Expressed alarm –
The secret was out –
The gulls and jackdaws knew.
Later, in long loops back and forth
The blackbirds flew.
As best I could I made repair
And then withdrew.
In their parallel world
Where's no need to forgive,
After a day or two their eggs had gone
Because of my intrusion.
Although, as I had hoped,
They had returned
And settled to their task, to live.

Animals in the Sun

Animals love to lie in the sun –
sheep, beside hedges,
after the early morning's graze;
cows do the same, and gently chew,
horses and their foals lie flat
in the centre of a field,
all slumber in the midday haze;
while in gardens,
cats curl in perfect corners
and stretch, and while they dream
of endless days
the blackbirds, safe,
rest on the grass their wings,
and laze.

Evening Light

As I cut the grass
The sun is sinking low,
And in the evening light
The periwinkles glow.

A crow of a sudden caws
As the day-noise fades,
Birdsong claims the still –
The chaffinches' cascades.

And as the air grows cooler,
On worm-hunt 'fore the night,
The blackbirds I encounter
'Neath the silent crow's home flight.

The Blackbirds' Absence

Companions in the evening light,
No longer hunting where I've mown,
Two pairs of adults and their young,
The blackbirds to the fields have flown.

'Though sparrows feed a second brood,
The blackbirds' absence lingers on,
While summer lasts they take their rest,
When they return, shall we have gone?

AUTUMN

" seagulls in the hurling gusts
soar high "

The Robin

Patient it waits, an unobtrusive friend,
To gardens come from edge of woodland shade;
Early in spring, while I weed or sow
The robin quietly sits upon a spade.

But later, with less lyrical a song
It warns intruders to its patch of lawn,
If neither yields to a show of red, though rare,
They battle, beak and claw, like daggers drawn.

When summer's past and nights are growing cold,
A time approaches which may not only be
The first, but as with other little birds,
Also the final winter it will see.

In the Wind

Swept about by winds, gale-force they say,
The birds at dawn are taking to the air.
Conifers billow, trees in hedgerows sway,
Sparrows, flung from roosts, fly low and fast
While starlings, in small groups, cut through the rain.
Geese fly alone, or form in twos or threes,
Jackdaws, from chimneys flushed, sway wide in crowds
And flirt with leaving for a place elsewhere.
Seagulls in the hurling gusts soar high
Or free-fall in the empty gaps between
And leave the sky, as now the garden's, bare.

The Kestrel

Still as stone, a statue in the air,
The kestrel hunts, screwed into the wind
Where the strength is, on the cliff's edge;
It feels the force, streaming through feathers of its wing.
Then, of a sudden, away from the sea,
As if on a calculated length of a kite's string,
It flies back to fix on a new place – motionlessly.

After the Wind

Another day; the sun is back again!
On lawn and rooftops glows its golden light;
Blue shows, through ink-black clouds and grey,
Picked out, the gliding gulls, with touch of white.
In calmer skies now jackdaws fly in pairs,
Active in hedge are blue tits and a wren,
Showers fall heavy on head and stiffened wing –
Blackbirds search for worm-food, e'en in rain.

The Collared Dove

From the chestnut tree it calls its mate,
Below the smoking cowl,
More gentle than a cuckoo's song,
Less haunting than the owl.

Patient in the cold it waits
As the morning passes by,
And through the window looks at me
With a dark and watchful eye.

The Goldcrest

Into a normal day, suddenly,
From somewhere else it came.
Wild and fluttery,
Coloured bright;
Moving swiftly along the wall,
A little bird with wings full-charged,
In purposed flight;
Darting and dancing
Through the branches of the quince
It lightly touched
But did not settle on;
Then, just as suddenly,
It was gone.

WINTER

" And join .... its life-mate as it
passes by "

Winter Dawn

Sparrows early, in a chill mist, from sleep
Disturbed, in a flutter about the hedge, twitter
And chip the stillness of the ice-cold air,
A blackbird curls a cadence, in a miracle of song
But frozen into silence, sings today no more;
Finches spare few notes, straying across the sky
Gulls wail a snatch of chorus, unrehearsed.
A starling sounds, but once, its practised flute
As from the remnants of my dreams I fly
To where the waders pipe along the shore.

Rooks in My Garden

Rooks in a raid,
Outsize birds in my garden
Among blackbirds and the rest,
Run, legs apart, to balance weight,
Back and forth, or, with outstretched wings,
Leap about on springs;
Too starved to dignify their gait.

In the Air

Seagulls float in winds from off the sea
And sail with outstretched wings across the sky –
Birds of the air, to prove their mastery there,
Together with the rooks and jackdaws vie.

But – sudden change – when clouds have frozen hard,
Stones of hail start falling from the sky
And clear the air; I ask but find not where
The birds have gone, I saw so lately fly.

In winter's night-cold, water turned to ice,
The little birds beneath an open sky,
Exposed to the air, while from my warmth I stare,
To kin cling close and do not question why.

Crows

Jackdaws in pairs and rooks in passing
Gather on roofs in windy weather,
All in black, each part of a crowd,
They rise on a gust and fly together.

A magpie plunders in shade on the lawn,
Shy of men, its white plumage ruffled,
While, awkward, on the ridge of a roof
A crow bends forward and sideways shuffles.

Back on *their* roof and close together,
As daylight darkens to black night,
They watch rooks flying, overhead –
A pair of jackdaws, sitting tight.

Winter Day

In the morning chill I wake
To clamour of geese;
In strings they pass across a sky
Pale blue, and rose, and cold.
Frost's painted on the lawn
And water's frozen, since break
Of day, the birds have fed –
Starlings strut, for leatherjackets stab,
Blackbirds peck 'neath apple trees,
Before my eyes they multiply,
A fieldfare, rich in dun and grey,
Darts with pointed beak like they,
While seagulls argue overhead.
But these feed hurriedly throughout the day,
Survival-bent, their silence keep
Till 'fore dim light, mid-afternoon,
When next I look – they've gone!
And found relief from cold, in sleep.

In the Rain

Wet drips down from roofs and sills,
Birds seem happy when it rains,
Running down their backs in rills,
Normality's resumed again.

They call a truce as clement weather
Monosyllabic talk allows,
Preen and shake their ruffled feathers,
Find permanence in here and now.

A jackdaw, in a manner casual
Barged from its perch, prepares to fly
And join, on hearing a quip-like call,
Its life-mate as it passes by.

Acknowledgement

While these poems draw on my own observations over many years, I should like to thank the RSPB Wildlife Enquiries team for its help with some of the facts.